XPRESSIT PUBLICATIONS

Philadelphia, PA
Copyright © 2015 by Arnita DeShields

All rights reserved. In accordance with the US Copyright Act of 1976, the scanning, uploading, and electronic sharing of any part of this book without the permission of the publisher is unlawful piracy and theft of the author's intellectual property. If you would like to use material from the book (other than for review purposes), prior written permission must be obtained by contacting the publisher. Thank you for your support of the author's rights.

Printed in the United States of America

Library of Congress Control Number
ISBN: 978-0-9714006-2-7

WATCH GOD MOVE

Arnita DeShields

CONTENTS

Dedication
Author's Note
Foreword
Introduction
Chapter 1 - The Storm is Passing Over
Chapter 2 - The Power of Prayer
Chapter 3 - I'm Still Standing
Chapter 4 - Don't Quit
Chapter 5 - Letting Go
Chapter 6 - I Got Joy
Chapter 7 - Our Children Have A Voice
Chapter 8 - Mighty Men Of Valor
Chapter 9 - Virtuous Women
Chapter 10 - Watch God Move
Poem of Encouragement - "Watch God Move"
10 Day Journal
Prayer of Salvation
Watch God Move in the life of Arnita DeShields
About the Author
Connect with the Author
About the Publisher

DEDICATION

Watch God Move is dedicated to my parents, the late(Ranzo DeShields) and Mary Elizabeth DeShields who always encouraged me to follow my dreams and to never give up. I'm so grateful for their love and support and I love them dearly. I am so proud of my dad, a Purple Heart recipient who carried a wounded soldier who cried out to him for help, across the battlefield in World War II.

"Honor your father and mother, which is the first commandment with promise." (Ephesians 6:2)

Watch God Move is also dedicated to my son, Joseph Emmanuel Cirksey. He has been a wonderful cheerleader during this assignment from God and refers to himself as my Advisor. I love him and I'm grateful for the blessing he has been in my life.

"See, children are a heritage from the Lord: and the fruit of the womb is his reward." (Psalm 127:3)

Author's Note

"I thank my God upon every remembrance of you." (Philippians 1:3)

Thank you Lord for all you have done for me and for birthing this book through me. Great is thy faithfulness!

Thank you, Prophet Todd Hall, for allowing the Lord to use you to speak to me about this book and more! I knew it was God speaking through you, because I only told God.

Thank you, Dorothy Goins, (CEO, Xpressit Publications) You came into my life and blessed me with your experience, love, prayers and helped me to finish strong!

To my Pastor, Reverend Harry Moore, Sr., thank you for covering me and my church family at Mount Olive Baptist Church.

Thank you to my family and friends. You all have impacted my life in some special way and I'm glad that I have been able to witness God moving in your life!

Foreword

I think everyone should read *Watch God Move*. It is an easy book to read, which is exactly what I look for in a book. No matter what your reading level is, no matter if you have a PHD or a GED, you will be able to understand and be inspired by the contents of *Watch God Move*.
 This book is real, relevant, refreshing and revitalizing. It will focus on everyday life, real situations and real people. Read and Watch God Move!

Grace and Peace,

Reverend Harry Moore, Sr. - Pastor
Mount Olive Baptist Church

INTRODUCTION

Watch God Move was birthed because of my own personal experiences of how God has come through for me, time and time again. I remember going to a Chinese restaurant in Philadelphia and being stuck up at gun point; one man held the door leading into the restaurant, while the other man held the front door with the gun pointed to my head. It was dark inside and they got the money, but I walked away with my life. God moved!

Some things I can't even explain, but I know it has been God moving and doing the impossible in my life.
If you are discouraged and feel like giving up, now is not the time for quitting. God did not forget about you and He will see you through anything. It is my hope and prayer that as you read some of my testimony and the testimonies of some others, that you will be uplifted, encouraged and will

see God move in your own life. Then, you will be able to pass your testimony on to someone else.

Some of you are waiting on a miracle, looking for God to deliver you and make your dreams a reality. He can do it. He is more than able to handle your situation. Fear not, because He is with you. This book will help you to stay focused on accomplishing your goals and making every dream a reality. It's a wonderful reminder of God's love and what He can do if you keep your eyes focused on Him.

In the end you win! I have included a 10 day journal with daily prayers in the back of this book so that you can record your experiences of how God has moved in your life. You will see each situation no matter how it looked, transform into a beautiful butterfly. Your crawling days are over! Get ready to spread your wings and fly! Watch God Move!

"For with God nothing shall be impossible!" (Luke 1:37)

"In the beginning God created the heaven and the earth. And the earth was without form, and void; and darkness was upon the face of the deep. And the Spirit of God moved upon the face of the waters." (Genesis 1: 1-2)

Chapter 1

The Storm Is Passing Over

Life is full of storms. Storms come and storms go but God is and has kept you through each one. Day by day we need God's light to shine on our dark situations. Life can hit you with some hard blows but if you continue to walk in the light of God, He will see you through any situation. It may not feel good or look good, but be encouraged by God's Word which states: "Weeping may endure for a night, but joy will come in the morning."

Jesus has come that you would have life and have it more abundantly. There is no storm that you are experiencing that you and God can't handle. When God moves, He will silence every demon and every force the enemy will attempt to bring your way. You must constantly remind yourself that

Jesus is the way, the truth and the life, and that no one comes to the Father except by Him. Walk in the light for it is a beautiful light.

God is willing to shine His love to any open vessel that is ready to receive. His love will calm any storm and give you the necessary direction that will lead you to a powerful victory. So be not weary in well doing, for in due season you shall reap if you faint not.

Hold on my brother and hold on my sister for a change is going to come. Some things you may never understand, so take it to the altar and leave it there. Let God move on your storm. Turn it over to the Lord and He will work it out.

There are so many great things God has in store for you. Your life is in His hands. Every storm provides a lesson that will lead you into many truths. You will have more wisdom if you walk in God's light. His timing is perfect and He will show you His plan if you would allow Him to do so.

Open up your heart and open up your mind to all God has in store for you.

As a single mother, I have had many financial struggles but I would always go to God in prayer and I remember one day stepping out of my car and looking down on the ground and there was money. It was as if God said here you go, here is a little something to let me know he saw my tears and he heard my cry. It was the answered prayer that I needed to build my faith and belief in God, that He had me and that I will come out of this financial storm.

I remember the water company sending me a letter indicating that they were unable to reach the valve in front of my home to turn off my water because it was blocked, and it was my responsibility to fix it or I will get additional fees. Well, the valve to turn off the water was never blocked and it was visible for anyone to see, but God moved. So God gave me enough time to pay the bill, but they still came and put a shut off notice on my door and documented their records in the water company that the water was off.

God moved again, and the water continue to run in spite of what steps were taken to shut it off.

No matter what financial storm or any storm you may be facing, God will protect you in the ship and get you safely to the other side of complete deliverance.

Our thoughts are not His thoughts and our ways are not His ways. You must lean and depend on God. He will never let you down. You are never alone with God on your side. He will never leave you or forsake you. In His arms you are protected and God will provide all your needs according to His riches in glory!

Life and death are in the power of the tongue. You must speak life to every dead situation. Speak life over that illness. You shall live and declare the works of the Lord. Speak life over your family and friends addicted to drugs. He came that you would have life and have it more abundantly. Speak life over that broken relationship. Remember the enemy comes to kill, steal and destroy.

Speak life over your finances. Is there anything too hard for God? No! Nothing is impossible if you believe. Believe on the Father, the Son and the Holy Ghost. Oh my! You are fully loaded! Believe that you can do all things through Christ that strengthens you. Don't be scared and don't be dismayed. God will take care of you. What appears to be difficult and challenging for you is easy for God!

Watch God move in the life of Tina Scott

Tina started off with nothing when she went into business with Signature Wedding bridal store and how she started doesn't look anything like where she is now with her own business known as Bride of Christ Robes.

In 1996, there was an ice storm and there was a flood in the basement of Tina's store. As a result of this, she faced a financial crisis because people could not even get to the store.

Her basement was covered in four inches of water. Tina was advised that she had to get the water out by way of the insurance claims representative. The plumber she had reached out to informed her that the water was fresh, and he did not know where the water came from.

Also, the water company could not figure out where the water came from; she did not use them for years.

Her fabrics were soaked and several patterns got wet. Her mortgage payment was $2,000 a month and she was four months behind. She had to bag up the fabric that was wet but it was never picked up; the tail of the wedding gowns got wet but the gowns were fine and she was able to wash the fabric and use it. The water went away and only the rugs and floors were wet. She received more in return with $40,000 coming from the insurance company, which took her business to the next level.

The insurance company recorded her statement three or four times because they could not figure out where the water came from or where the water went.

Then, out of obedience to God, she started to dress his Brides in the ministry. She started making robes and to kick off her business she became a vendor at a National AME Convention for nine days in St. Louis with over 400 vendors. She thought she was in a bad spot because for three days she received no business. Tina was devastated because she took all her money and invested in this trip.

Then God moved a wall that was located next to the dining area and everyone had to go pass her table entering and leaving the dining area.

She started with a mix up in her application for vending, not making any sales, to having the best location for vending, 80 robes ordered, and today her business services over 5,000 women throughout the world.

Tina said she kept hearing not by power, nor by might but by His Spirit and kept saying He moved the wall! Tina was obedient, she stepped on faith and she watched God move!

"For with God nothing shall be impossible!" (Luke 1:37)

"In the beginning God created the heaven and the earth. And the earth was without form, and void; and darkness was upon the face of the deep. And the Spirit of God moved upon the face of the waters." (Genesis 1: 1-2)

CHAPTER 2

The Power of Prayer

Prayer changes things. I don't know about you, but God knows and He understands everything about you. Everyone needs someone to talk to, so why not talk to God. Tell him about your troubles, your problems, your tests and your trials.

In July of 1997, my dad, Ranzo DeShields passed away and the grief that I experienced was not healthy at all, but God healed my heart. I was strong during the care giving process and lasted until the home-going service, but when it was all over the reality of my dad's death really sank in. My dad fought a great battle with cancer and was diagnosed with Hodgkin's Disease. He fought a good battle just like he did when he was in WWII. So I commuted back and forth from New Jersey to Philadelphia to care for my dad. I took him back and forth to his appointments and made sure I was there for his procedures with my mother, many times by my side.

I remember after he passed away I was initially standing at the altar during prayer for Sunday service, but as the Holy Spirit moved on me, I kneeled down and God began the work of healing my heart and removing heaviness that can come along with grief. I had to take the burden of grief to him in prayer. I had to go to God in prayer to help me with care giving; my dad would sometimes fall out in my hands because he was so weak from chemo treatment, but God allowed me to catch him and get him into the house.

I remember the first time my dad passed away in the hospital and I stretched forth my hand towards His room as the medical staff worked on Him and prayed. I asked God to raise him up like he raised Lazarus from the dead and He granted my petition. I saw a miracle – God moved! When it was all over and my dad went home to be with Jesus, it was God who gave me the strength that I needed to continue on. I surrendered to God in prayer and God moved!

God has the answer to every situation you are facing. You can go to God in prayer. He is a heart fixer and a mind regulator. He is a redeemer and a restorer and there is nobody like Him! You can call Him anytime and any day. He is always able and available to hear your humble cry.

Talk to God about the death of a loved one, talk to Him about your children and talk to him about your dreams. You can talk to God when you are sad, mad or even glad. He will accept you just as you are, be it weary, wounded or worn; it does not matter what condition you are in, talk with Him and

Watch GOD Move   19

He will talk with you. Have a conversation with Him about love, peace and joy, hope and health, success and stress – no matter what you have to say – God wants to hear, respond and He will answer by and by. Just have a little talk with Jesus for there is power in His name.

Praise God in advance for change. He loves to hear the sound of praise in your prayer. Add some worship with your praise and watch God move. God wants to help you as a single mother and give you double for your shame. God wants to help you get through college and pay every bill, with money left over for all the meals.

Sometimes you may think that God is not listening but try Him and you will see that He will not just listen but respond and meet your every need. I hear you saying, my needs are so great and problems are too and I wonder if God will ever see me through. What a mighty God we serve. He sits high and he looks low.

There is nothing too hard for God. Trust and obey and He will show you the way out of depression, out of low self-esteem, clarity for a confused mind. There is power in prayer. Prayer changes things.

I love to talk with my Lord and Savior for He is sovereign. So many times I didn't know what to say and I didn't even know where to go, or even what to do, but when I turned it over to Jesus, He made everything alright.

Prayer will turn your test into a testimony. Greater is He that is in you, than He that is in the world. You have the victory through the power of prayer.

Watch God Move in the life of Tyre Brant and the life of Elder Emma Brant

Tyre is the son of Elder Brant and was born in December of 1983 and Elder Brant's Mom passed away in December of 1981.

Tyre was born with a kidney disease; acid spilled into his blood at 11 weeks old. He had a cyst on his kidneys that could not be removed with surgery and the doctors said he would not live past 7 months old. Elder Brant did not believe it, she trusted God and prayed. She told God, "If you give me my son's life, I will she give you my life."

Tyre was blessed with a kidney from his father and later had a reaction from medicine that caused him to have seizures. Elder Brant consulted with God once again and she was instructed to take Tyre off one of the medications and the doctors honored her request. Tyre never had another kidney rejection or anymore seizures since December of 1988.

God kept His promise and God knew Elder Brant's heart. On July 31, 1987, she gave God her life and she was also delivered from smoking. She had smoked from age 14 to age 34.

Elder Brant says, "All you have to do is ask!"

"For with God nothing shall be impossible!"(Luke 1:37)

"In the beginning God created the heaven and the earth. And the earth was without form, and void; and darkness was upon the face of the deep. And the Spirit of God moved upon the face of the waters." (Genesis 1: 1-2)

CHAPTER 3

I'm Still Standing

Have you ever had a season when there was nothing but test after test. Some days, months or weeks will be a little more challenging than others. I remember when I lost my brother but not permanently. Grief and loss can at times be unbearable but with God on your side there is strength to get you through every time.

My brother, Wilbert, passed away at age 60. I watched my brother battle situations in prison, all types of legal matters, from attorneys to court cases, financial problems, and all types of illness with multiple symptoms. I never saw someone fight like him – he was an inspiration to both me and my entire family.

He was walking, talking and caring for himself up until the night before he passed away.

Watching a loved one fight for their life can also be challenging, but God. When God is in it – no matter what is going on – He will always have the final say. While my brother Wilbert was fighting in the hospital, I was still fighting for my brother to be released from prison to home for medical care and although he never made it to his natural home – he did accept Jesus before he passed away. I was also grateful that we were able to have his home-going service at a chapel in Philadelphia, and the brothers from the prison in Huntingdon, Pennsylvania really touched me with a big beautiful hand-made sympathy card that included all their signatures and special messages to our family.

My dad passed away in July 1997 and then my brother at age 60. I watched my brother battle all types of illness and multiple symptoms.

When you are facing life situations that are out of your hands, it is at these times when you must remember whose life your hands are in. God's hands are loving, gentle but strong, peaceful and secure. Everything you need is in God's hands. Our loved ones are safe in His hands and our lives are safe in His hands. That's why we can be still and see the salvation of the Lord.

When my brother passed away I was both shocked and sad. I had so many emotions that came all at once. It is at these times that you must place your mind in God's hands. I got the call and now had the responsibility of telling others in my family, nobody but God. He always comes through. He is a very present help in times like these.

After I received the 4th call, I remember pulling over to the side of the road and calling on the name of Jesus. Sometimes you have to stop and call His name. It did not matter who was on the line or who saw me, I needed to call His name. There is so much power in His name. As tears began to roll down my face and with a heavy heart, I was reminded of the good news in the midst of it all and that is, and will always be, that my brother accepted Christ on a Sunday morning about a week before he passed away. I'm smiling right now because the enemy, thought he had Him but he got away. He got a new address, a home sweet home over in glory! And, I'm still standing and my family is standing too!

I offered salvation to my brother and was surprised when he told me he was not saved. He grew up with Bible study in our home and he knew about God but did not know God for himself.

You can go to church every day, sing on the choir and do several good deeds but are you saved. Do you know that you must be born again? I was saying a prayer with my brother Wilbert and my sister Elaine before we ended our visit and was lead to stop and ask Wilbert if he was saved and he said no, and that no response promptly turned into a yes response. Wilbert was saying yes to God's will and to His way. Nothing else really matters but Jesus. You must be born again. This is how you stand. This is how you make peace with God.

You may not even love yourself and forgot all about loving God. But know this, God is love and love conquers all. Didn't He wake you up this morning and start you on your way? You are still standing. You have yet another opportunity to tell someone that Jesus saves before its too late because tomorrow is not promised to any of us. We must choose Christ today.

There is a person assigned to you that will say yes to Christ so stand with confidence and have no fear for the Lord is near. Romans 10: 9 and 10 states, "If thou shalt confess with thy mouth the Lord Jesus, and shalt believe in thine heart that God hath raised him from the dead, thou shalt be saved."

Watch God move in the life of Dorothy Goins

Imagine feeling like you're always losing instead of winning even after God has spoken to you through a prophetic word and assured you that something good is soon to happen and you know he made you some promises but you see no signs of anything He has spoken. That's how Dorothy Goins felt when the first major loss hit her.

The death of her beloved mother, Jessie Mae Coleman happened suddenly in the wee hours of May 19, 2013. The ride to the hospital felt like the longest ride as Dorothy drove with her sister, Rebecca Coleman and her daughter, Ciara Goins riding along with her over to the hospital to see about Jessie Mae after receiving a phone call from the E.R. doctor at Einstein Hospital located in Philadelphia, Pa.

Jessie Mae was diabetic and was diagnosed with congestive heart failure because of the diabetes. Within the time-frame of two years, she had suffered two mild heart attacks, so Dorothy was moved to fear on that drive over to the hospital. She had witnessed her mother having the second heart attack and that was the first thought she had on that silent ride over to the hospital. Not wanting to alarm her sister or her daughter, she buried that thought quickly and prayed quietly on what felt like the longest ride ever.

In the wee hours of that Sunday morning, after arriving at the hospital, Dorothy, her sister and her daughter along with their brother-in law all received the unbearable news that Jessie Mae Coleman had passed away. The news cut through Dorothy like a knife. It was not until the next day that they found out that the cause of death was definitely from a massive heart attack. This was the hardest news to bear and the most difficult to accept.

Dorothy sat crying in the lobby of Einstein hospital alongside her six sisters, trying to console seventeen grand-children which included her son and her daughter, after calling all the family to the hospital. Watching them fall to pieces as the news was disclosed to them all was all the more painful. They sat together trying to wrap their minds around the sudden and unexpected death of the one person that meant the world to all of them. This was hard for Dorothy and her family to understand.

Even more so for Dorothy, because she had just had a dream that morning that led her to believe God was already warning her of what was to come but she couldn't put it together. She remembered being led to pray for all the grandchildren and not understanding why she was doing that.

Just three months earlier, Dorothy and her sisters hosted a surprise 70th birthday celebration for Jessie Mae Coleman. The celebration consisted of all their mother's friends and family who had traveled a long way to share this special time with this beautiful and loving woman who had impacted them in some special way. People showed up that Jessie Mae had not seen in a very long time. Who knew this would be her last celebration with loved ones and special friends. Who knew this would be the last celebration that Jessie Mae's daughters would have with her.

This transition was hard. In fact, it took a lot to worship and praise God in the same manner and with the same perseverance that Dorothy had before this dreadful day. Dorothy knew God was yet still faithful even unto death but it was the absence of her mother that took a toll on her. Her heart was heavy and having to watch her whole family hurt was not easy at all.

It was through this phase of hurt, loss and emotional suffering that more hurt found its way into what was already an emotional downward spiral for Dorothy.

At a time when the loss was so great and the grief was so encompassing, Dorothy thought friends would be available, especially those who had grew up around them. That was not the case. People were unreachable and not reaching out to her like she had expected. After the funeral, it felt like everyone had disappeared.

When she went to church, there was no peace there. Some that she believed to be friends there had begun to treat her differently and were less trust worthy than she had known at the time. Being there was now uncomfortable. She would enter the sanctuary and try hard to worship and tears would come from out of nowhere.

Some days she preferred just staying home and when she did, she got calls from church friends who thought they were helping, when in reality, they were not. It was hard being in the same place where her mother's funeral took place. Dorothy felt so lost without her mother. Grief had gripped her hard. Suddenly, her life had changed. God called Dorothy out of her church.

Prior to her mother's death, Dorothy had been laid off from her job and that transition was good for them both because it had given Dorothy extra time with her mother to care for her and to take her to church. It gave Dorothy time to pray with her mother and to be available for all the doctor visits and it was Dorothy who God had chosen to pray over her mother when she went into the hospital and the stays were extended every time.

Through this difficult time, God provided the strength that Dorothy needed to help her mother through her fearful times when doctors were doing major tests on her heart. Dorothy was there with her mother holding her hand through every test. It was at these times that she was not aware what God was doing through her, let alone what God was doing for her. He was giving her time with her mother. He was giving her special time.

So imagine, how Dorothy felt one month later after her mother's passing when unemployment suddenly cut her off without any prior warning. She lost her only source of income. The money she had saved up was now being used to pay her bills. Within three months, her savings were depleted and the next loss was her car. The finance company took her car because she fell three months behind. Dorothy prayed and God sent people to Dorothy who just gave her money without her asking, which helped her get her car back.

Even still the losses kept coming because Dorothy was not able to find employment right away. Standing on her faith, Dorothy continued to pray while struggling to pay her rent in the house she was living in, maintaining other bills and not sure where anything was coming from in this trying circumstance. And to make matters worse, another death hit the family hard.

Five months after her mother's passing, Dorothy and her family got the news that their mother's oldest brother died in hospice and no one had notified the family. He was cremated without the family's knowledge. The losses kept coming. And so did the dreams Dorothy was having.

Several months later, Dorothy's paternal grandmother who she was very close to in relationship passed away. More grief encompassed her life but Dorothy kept on believing God would turn things around. She kept reminding God of His promises to her. She was no longer in the same church and she had followed God's prompting to leave and go to a new church which she did. Shortly after, God blessed Dorothy in the temporary job assignment she was in to full hire status as a permanent employee. God was closing doors and opening new doors. When she was hired on her job, Dorothy recalled the dream she had one morning where she'd seen herself going in one door and out another door.

One more loss came before things turned around for her good. Without warning, her landlord filed an eviction with the courts stating Dorothy had fell behind in her rent for two months, and even though she had caught up what she owed from losing her income, he deceitfully filed that false claim against her.

Dorothy was asleep in her prayer room when God called out to her one morning in the wee hours and He spoke to her about her leaving that home. God lovingly said to her, "All this is my doing beloved. Even what's happening with your landlord. I have a new home for you and a new beginning for you and your daughter."

Dorothy did a lot of weeping and lost a lot of sleep in the months to come. In the span of all the losses she suffered, the enemy attacked her finances and he attacked her daughter's mind. While attempting to get through her own grieving process, her daughter slipped into deep depression while she was away in college, after the death of her best friend who passed after a four year battle with colon cancer. Her daughter had to come home on medical leave from her college two months before Dorothy's mother passed.

Nights were long as Dorothy's daughter woke her up constantly during the panic attacks she was experiencing. Dorothy felt so alone as she walked this path with her daughter, praying over her and attending hospitals and watching her daughter suffer. But yet and still, she stood on her faith. She saw God move through every obstacle she was facing with her grief and with her financial downfalls and this was one area in her life that she was determined to believe God would fix. Healing belongs to us all and it takes standing on God's word and walking it out with Him. Dorothy saw her daughter's healing and not the mental illness that was diagnosed by the psychiatrist and therapists who evaluated her daughter.

Many people did not understand what Dorothy was going through and their words were discouraging but Dorothy refused to believe people, she chose to believe the report God gave and what He had already promised her.

God summoned Dorothy to leave her home in October of 2014 and directed her to move in with a best friend who had invited her to move with her until she was able to get on her feet. God directed her path and He stood with her in the court and she never had to face that landlord. She never had to pay him anything. He lost and Dorothy won. Her daughter was put on a road to recovery through assistance from mental health programs and counseling and today Dorothy stands on every promise God has made to her.

It was on the first day of the new year (2015) while laying in bed, Dorothy saw a vision that looked more like a dream and in it she saw her daughter's mind being healed. It is that vision that she grabbed a hold of and decided that day that there was no room for doubt. God is a promise keeper.

Within five months of moving out her home, God opened the doors for Dorothy. On her mother's birthday, (2/28/15) God blessed her with a new home and four months after her move, God opened another door and blessed her with a new job making double the amount of her last salary. God gave Dorothy double for her troubles.

"For with God nothing shall be impossible!" (Luke 1:37)

"In the beginning God created the heaven and the earth. And the earth was without form, and void; and darkness was upon the face of the deep. And the Spirit of God moved upon the face of the waters." (Genesis 1: 1-2)

CHAPTER 4

Don't Quit

So many times you asked yourself is it really worth it, can I go on, will I make it. I will press toward the mark for the prize of the high calling in Christ. He really does know how much you can bear. God saw the trouble before the trouble saw you and He remains true to His word. His word will come to pass in your life whether you like it or not.

You can't quit now. You are closer than you think to your turn around.

We all face strongholds in life but you have control over that hold and you can break free. How do you break free? Every time you fall, get up and dust yourself off, hold your head up and throw your hands up in praise to God. God is not through blessing you. Even when we fall from the cares and temptations in life, He is still right there to catch us, caress us and call us to a deeper dimension in Him.

You can't quit. Your faith is on the line and He is ready to battle every demon of doubt that comes to discourage you. Doubt has no place on the path that God has laid for you. Your foundation is sure and strong. Nothing or no one can turn you around now. Now is the time that you surround yourself with the word of God even more. Study night and day. Don't question God, for a good soldier never quits.

I had to remind myself not to quit when I applied to the University of Pennsylvania School of Social Work. The first time I applied I did not get accepted, but I tried again and my second time I did get accepted. Was it challenging and did I have some moments of discouragement, frustration and more. Yes, but I refused to quit. When unhealthy grief began to raise its head – I could have thrown in the towel, but I refused to quit.

My first intern was in Hospice and one of my responsibilities was to help create the bereavement department. I finally had to face the pain I felt in my father's death and all the emotions of the care giving process that I never dealt with in the past, but I chose not to do it alone.

I was not going to fail out of Penn and you had to get a grade of a B or better. I was watching other students drop out or go part-time and I made a vow to myself and God that I would not be in that number. I did get help with counseling and the sessions were a blessing; I walked across that stage with tears rolling down my eyes, one hand was holding my degree and the other hand I raised in the air giving God total praise. Maybe you feel like quitting right now or you got rejected. Try again. Don't quit – even if you have to seek out help. Everyone needs someone. God has given us counselors so that we do not have to suffer in silence, and it's alright that counselors receive counsel.

Sometimes your mind and your body get tired. Take a break and don't be blind to His many blessings, but be bold and bless His name for blessing you. Breathe hope again, for it's not over. You may be down but you are not out. I thought I had to be out of my apartment more than once because I just did not have the income. Eviction notices came but each time, God prevailed.

I remember going into court for an eviction hearing and the representative for the apartment was not present and the judge said case dismissed. I remember sitting in a network meeting and a sister who I did not even meet, blessed me with a check that cleared; and it was enough to cover my rent with money left over for other bills. I was ready to give up many times because of my financial struggles but God consistently has moved on my behalf.

You may be in a bad relationship that is filled with turmoil and today is your turning point. Today is your day to smile again and by the grace of God you are still here – you can't quit! The case is not closed but the celebration has already begun. A celebration of a champion – yes that is you!

Don't quit on God, don't quit on yourself and don't quit on those who love you. You are not alone – the Holy Spirit will guide you, no matter how long the situation has gone on, it will not stop your progress! Your prayer will be answered and God will point you in the right direction. Your steps are anointed. When you speak, show up or say what God has given you to say – don't quit!

You can face your worry and confusion because it will not stop you. The prize is great and the price was already paid on Calvary. You are covered with protection, power and purpose. Your dream must come to pass, your business must prosper, your family will come together; there is so much to be fulfilled – quitting is not the answer. Yes you can and yes you will shatter anger and defeat suicide because you are a treasure that God wants to use and he does not lie. The truth will remove every conflict and make clear every connection. Favor comes on two feet – the right relationships are critical for your journey – one can chase a thousand and two ten thousand. Quitting is not an option!

Watch God move in the life of Ty Ryans-Mease

Ty worked as an accountant with a financial company from 2004-2011 and in 2011 he was laid off. He consistently received a salary increase in this position but soon found himself unemployed. Ty did not give up because the bills kept coming in. He worked in a temporary position and kept looking for employment and in July 2015 he was looking at positions openings on Indeed.com and came across a Senior Staff Accountant position at the same company. Ty applied for the position and got the job. His current boss is his previous supervisor. Now with the title of Manager, he is in the same department, with the same co-workers, the same position and with the salary he had when he was laid off.

I remember him posting a prayer request on Facebook requesting that everyone cover him in prayer and the response was overwhelming in the support that he received. I was not surprised because every week, he would request prayer request on Facebook and one day I sent him mine. My prayer request was that I finish this book and I asked what was his prayer request and his request was to find employment. Well God has moved and answered both of our prayers, and for that I am grateful!

Ty shared that God has not forgotten about you and encourages all to continue to put your trust in Him. Rejection from a job is not the end of the world – it simply means God has something better for you. Keep God first and everything will fall into place.

"For with God nothing shall be impossible!" (Luke 1:37)

"In the beginning God created the heaven and the earth. And the earth was without form, and void; and darkness was upon the face of the deep. And the Spirit of God moved upon the face of the waters." (Genesis 1: 1-2)

CHAPTER 5

Letting Go

Letting go can be hard but is possible. All things are possible to them that believe. You must believe God first and foremost. He has given you power to let go. It may be a person or situation in your past or even your present – it does not matter when, where or with who the situation occurred – you still have the power to close the door and never open it again. I know that it is possible because I had to let go of some relationships, and when I let go, God moved the hurt, disappointment, stabilized my emotions and healed my heart.

This process of letting go will have some peaks and valleys. You must be committed and covered in prayer. You must be focused, faithful and fearless. So many things have already happened that you don't understand and there is no need to try and figure it out. Your past was a great stepping stone for your future. Your past was preparation that was not planned but necessary for your elevation. So many lessons learned –

through the good, the bad and the ugly. Some stuff just will not fit in your future.

Wherever God is taking you – you have no choice but to let it go. Maybe it's drugs, porn, prostitution, unforgiveness, bitterness and other negative strongholds that will wipe out and pollute your life or your future – you must guard your heart and your mind.

Letting go gives you access to a new beginning. Relationships have been hindered because you allow people and situations to have a dwelling place that God desires first. Haven't you made enough wrong turns that have taken you into a direction not of God and His will for your life. Our thoughts are not His thoughts. God sits high but He looks low. You may be in a low place right now and have difficulty of finding a way out. Every turn you make leads you to a dead end, but don't worry what God has for you, is for you. You are covered by His unconditional love.

Letting go means moving closer to God and His plans. God will order your steps to everything you shall need. He has not forgotten about you. He cares and He has your best interest in mind at all times.

Letting go is a good thing. You have been in bondage too long. Deep in your heart you knew something was wrong in that relationship or situation but you held on at all cost. You lost your self-esteem, confidence, security and so much more in trying to hold on. When you are surrounded by unhealthy people and situations, it affects every part of you. You can lose everything, including yourself. Letting go is a valuable step towards wholeness. God will take all the broken pieces of your life and put you back together again. He is the potter and you are the clay.

I had to let go of a marriage of twenty one years that was no longer healthy or safe. I had to make a decision that would impact every area of my life as well as my child. I realized my self-worth and knew that I deserved much better than how I was being treated by my husband. I had to let go of being concerned with how people may think or feel about my decision. I had to let go of worrying about how long I was in the marriage or thinking I needed to stay because I have a child and the money wasn't there. I had to trust God, let go and believe that God was going to help me on another journey of healing and freedom in Him.

So my divorce became final and I relocated with the necessary items in my car and I have not looked back. Single life has its moments, but I have more peace, new opportunities to serve God and raise my son in a healthy environment.

Letting go gives you access to a fresh start. You can depend on God. He will see you through every loss and every mistake. We must take full responsibility for some of the situations in our past. In doing so, make the situation worthwhile and learn from your mistakes. Learning your contribution to your demise will change you for the better. You live and you learn. What is life if you don't learn? Life is what you make it.

You are worthy of the best, so never settle for less. There is something in your past that was of lesser value. God always wants you to have His best. He always wants more for you. God's will be done on earth as it is in heaven. So don't worry about what people may say. Stay in God's will.

You can't let go unless you forgive. Forgiveness will set the captive free. You have to forgive yourself. Maybe you are holding on to something you did ten years ago or even on yesterday. You can only move forward by releasing yourself. The hurt and pain of what was said and done can only keep you in prison if you allow it. It's time to break free! If you are not able to talk directly with the person you must forgive. It's okay. Thank God for the altar. You can take it to Him in prayer!

Watch God move in the life of William and Tamika Haynes

William and Tamika let go of their familiar surroundings in Philadelphia and moved to Texas without either of them having a job. They had crazy faith! There was a period when they didn't have any money coming in at all. I mean absolutely no income and God would put it on someone's heart to send them a check; and then tell them to give to someone else in need out of their savings.

Tamika said, "It was not easy for them, but God taught us how to totally depend on Him for every need to be supplied and although some days things were so tight, God never let us go without! God is truly Jehovah Jireh!"

Tamika wants you to know that God is real and He does care in the midst of your situation!

"For with God nothing shall be impossible!" (Luke 1:37)

"In the beginning God created the heaven and the earth. And the earth was without form, and void; and darkness was upon the face of the deep. And the Spirit of God moved upon the face of the waters." (Genesis 1: 1-2)

CHAPTER 6

I Got Joy

In spite of everything that you have been through, you still have joy. You have had many life situations that could have taken you out with sadness and depression but God said "No! Not on His watch." The joy of the Lord shall be your strength. You can put a smile on your face when you know victory has your name on it and God has the final say.

God does not want you to live in defeat and be miserable. He wants your joy to be complete in Him. Misery does not qualify to be a part of your life, so close the door on it and say hello sunshine – joy unspeakable full of glory.

I had to close the door on sadness when I had a miscarriage. I was devastated, I cried and was disappointed that my child passed away. I remember my Pastor calling me to see if I was okay and I told him I was, but I was hurting on the inside. I believe I was about to slip into a depression, but God had another plan. I was able to heal and experience joy again. I was blessed with another child, my son Joseph Emmanuel, who is a constant reminder that God is with me.

You know you got joy when all hell has broken loose and after the dust has settled you are still standing with a smile on your face. Some people will look at you crazy because they really don't understand, but when God gives you joy, He will confuse the enemy. Joy is sacred and you must guard it with your life.

You got joy when your walk turns into a skip. God has given you a special step because you are bubbling over with joy. It can't be contained but shared with others. Your joy is contagious and negativity can't contaminate it and people can't take it away. You got joy!

Joy gives you satisfaction and an assurance that everything will be alright. You can't worry when you are a winner, no matter what! You will laugh when you should be crying, you persevere when you should give up. There are no frowns, only smiles. Why? Because you know that God is more than able to do all things but fail.

You got joy when you look at death and grief and decide to live a resurrected life right here on earth. No disease, no loss of a loved one, no illness can take you out. You remind yourself that God is a healer. He is a Balm and Gilead that will heal you from the inside out.

You have seen God move every time and you still wondered, thought or questioned Him. He constantly shows up and comes through for you and for me. Joy is an expression of how grateful you are for all God is, and all the many blessings you receive daily. You recognize God has demonstrated His love in your life over and over again. You could have been dead and gone but you got back up. God showed up in the nick of time and on time. If you can't relate to this joyful experience, hold on because it's not over for you! You will no longer speculate but participate!

Watch God move in the life of Dale Croxton

Dale was called a miracle baby. She was born in 1948 and weighed only 3 lbs. Dale stayed in the hospital over a month before she had a safe weight.

Miracles continued in Dale's life even when her leg fell under a boat and she saw her bone come through the flesh of her leg. When her husband pulled her leg out, her leg was fine. Dale was also healed from cancer. Dale has joy because over and over again God came through for her, and she appreciates everything He has done! She really understands what it means to count it all joy!

"For with God nothing shall be impossible!" (Luke 1:37)

"In the beginning God created the heaven and the earth. And the earth was without form, and void; and darkness was upon the face of the deep. And the Spirit of God moved upon the face of the waters." (Genesis 1: 1-2)

CHAPTER 7

Our Children Have A Voice

When children rise in the morning or when they lie down to sleep at night, they are speaking. Stop, look and listen because their voice matters. They speak loud and clear with the things they do and the things they say.

They are speaking about love. Love is passion, love is an emotion, love is a gift and love is a treasure indeed. We can't stop loving our children; they are growing each and every day – they need us! Are you available?

There is a child right now going through bullying at school. He or she does not know what to do, where to go or who to turn to. Bullying is painful experience for a child to handle and powerful wound for a young soul. But God's promise for our children is protection, direction and wisdom. They are never alone. God has angels all around them. The enemy can't have their minds. A price was paid on Calvary. Our children will be courageous and victorious. No contact from the enemy will control or destroy them, or hinder the positive impact that we have on their lives. So, say a prayer, hold on tight, because bullying, drugs, violence and more must take a flight!

Our children need to spend their time wisely. They need time to listen, walk, talk and play. Our children need time to dream! We must hold their hands, guide them along life's way. Our children have a destiny and so much promise to fulfill! If you listen to their voice, you will hear the preacher, the teacher, the judge, the doctor, the lawyer, the President and so much more. All their dreams will become a reality in spite of every obstacle, test or trial – Watch God Move!

Our children have fears, some have been hurt by life situations and people too, but somehow with the help of God, they always get through. When you listen to their voice, change will come for their good and the enemy will flee because he is out for no good! Our children will not fall into the enemy plots and schemes, because Christ blood has covered both them and their dreams.

We all know that our children need our help – they experience so many diseases, sickness and an attack on their hearts. But God can see their hearts and meet each of their needs for healing, joy and great self-esteem. My son, Joseph, swallowed a coin when he was a toddler and we rushed him to the hospital as he was gasping for air. I remembered praying for him until he settled down but was still concerned. Joseph made it to the hospital alive and although the coin had to be removed from his chest area, it did miss his heart. The surgery was a success and my son was, and is still healthy and well. No weapon formed against our children shall prosper. Watch God move!

So get involved and make a difference in a child's life – they need you to participate and take a stand! Stand against abuse and neglect, hate, rejection and racism and respond to their voice and they will respond to yours. Oh what an opportunity awaits both you and yours, to touch a child with love delivered by God, straight from above. Our children are wonderful vessels with so much to offer the world so we must cover them and be the best examples of what God has in store, and remind them daily that He is the one they should always adore. There will be no regrets for what our children will do or say!

Watch God move in the life of Sharrod Williams

Sharrod was running around playing with his friends at the age of 9 years old. He went to sleep one night in September of 1992 and woke up very sick. Sharrod was so sick; he did not recognize who he was or where he was. His mom, Vendetta, had to rush him to St. Christopher's Hospital for Children.

When Sharrod and his mother arrived at St. Christopher's, Sharrod was unable to walk. He was screaming his legs hurt. He had to be carried into the emergency room where they rushed him back to be treated. Doctors quickly placed Sharrod on antibiotics after diagnosing him with Shigella. After about 15-20 minutes of receiving the antibiotics, Sharrod's mom noticed a reaction to his body and quickly notified the doctors.

The doctors came to check on Sharrod and after noticing his body's reaction to the antibiotics they quickly scrambled calling for more staff, IV Machines and medications. When Sharrod's mom was able to speak with the doctors, they explained to her that her son did not have Shigella. It was explained to her that he had a disease known as Bacterial Meningitis and it was stated that he might not make it through the night.

When Sharrod's mother was able to enter her son's room he had an estimate of about 13 machines connected to him. She went to his bed side. Being a strong believer in God, she yelled at her son to fight. She would not give up on him and would not allow her son to give up either. With the grace of God, Sharrod made it through that night and other nights. The doctors were puzzled and did not know how this kid was surviving. They continued to tell Sharrod's mom not get to excited because he still may not make it. After a few weeks, Sharrod was still alive and fighting hard. Look at God.

Though Sharrod was surviving, the disease still continued to eat away at his body, turning his arms and legs black. The doctors prepared him for surgery explaining to his mother and grandmother that Sharrod most likely would lose his finger tips and toes due to the fact that the disease stopped the blood flow to that area of his body.

After the surgical procedure on Sharrod, the doctors came back to his mother and said, while they were trying to get rid of the dead tissue in Sharrod's limbs, they noticed more and more infection that traveled into his bones. Because of the spread of infection, the only way they could save her son's life was by amputating his legs slightly above the knees and his arms slightly below the elbow. Sharrod's mom did not care; all she wanted was her son. God made it possible for Sharrod to fight a good fight and he beat the odds, surviving a disease which has killed others in the first 24hrs. The disease may have taken his arms, legs, kidneys, and partial hearing in his right ear but it did not stop Sharrod.

God made it possible for Sharrod to earn a degree from Chestnut Hill College in Human Services. Sharrod is working full time at the IRS and drives himself daily. He is married with three children and he is a deacon. Every day you can see Sharrod living life and "Pressing on towards the mark" as Paul stated in Philippians.

"For with God nothing shall be impossible!" (Luke 1:37)

"In the beginning God created the heaven and the earth. And the earth was without form, and void; and darkness was upon the face of the deep. And the Spirit of God moved upon the face of the waters." (Genesis 1: 1-2)

Chapter 8

Mighty Men of Valor

Men who love God display both bravery and wisdom. They not only look out for their families but look out for others too. Sometimes they get frustrated when life trials come their way, but they stand every test knowing that success is their way. So they hold their heads high and fight to the end because victory is not an option – it's a must that they win!

    I want to pause right here and honor my Dad, Ranzo DeShields, who is a purple heart recipient. In WWII, he had crossed the battlefield and there was a wounded soldier crying out to my Dad to come back and get him and my Dad did just that. He sacrificed his life and went back to get him – he picked up the soldier and carried him across his shoulder to safety. This has been a great example for me to follow and although, I may never have to carry someone across a battlefield, my goal is to help whenever God gives me the opportunity to do so. I appreciate and salute all those who have served our country both the past and present – your labor of love is not in vain. You and my dad are mighty men of valor! Watch God move!

So many men have faced pain, sorrow, and agony all at one time, but their response in faith has gotten them through each time. They sometimes wondered if they would make it because they experienced tragedy and problems on every hand, but they knew that who was inside of them would cause them to win and continue to stand! Men on the move don't have time to waste because they believe in God as the only way. So they may smile in spite of their test because they know the reality will rule in their favor, if they just keep the faith.

Men who face drugs and alcohol may struggle to break the addiction or walk away from the temptation, but their faith in God continues to encourage them to walk the distance. Men have problems in their homes and many other relationships bring doubt and concern, but they always remember the cross where Christ Jesus died! When men think of Christ and the authority they were given to defeat the enemy they shake themselves and soar over every obstacle and beat every opposition. When God is moving, it does not matter what may come their way, because mighty men know they serve a mighty God!

When men watch God move and make their dreams a reality and make their homes like a heart filled with love they have no choice but to thank Him for He is God alone. Men will recognize God moving and may not doubt for a little while, but will not stay in that place long because their God is too great!

Men realize more and more that with God the center of their joy, the road may get rough and the going may get tough, but with God on their side, they can stay on the ride. A mighty man of valor is determined to conquer every mental disorder or distraction. They understand that the peace of God cannot and will not be denied in their life. Over and over again they have watched God move on their minds because they have kept their mind on Jesus. When you keep your focus on God, the battle of the mind will not only have a positive outcome but another brother will be helped along the way.

Men who watch God move know that they can let go of their past and move forward with honor, dignity and humility. They know they may fall in relationships, fall in their finances, fall in ministry, and fall in whatever life may bring their way. But they also know that they can get back up and try again. Men who watch God and know that God will move understand that falls are a trick of the enemy that God can and will use for His glory. So they find a way with tears rolling down their face and they get back up and keep running this race.

Men who watch God move love Him and show Him! They have nothing but gratitude. The more men thank God, the more God will show up and show out!

Men who see God moving, refuse to quit. They refuse to give in because they know that God is more than able to change and transform any life issue or situation. At some point a man was homeless and watched God provide him with a home. Another man was single and God gave him a lovely wife. Another man was divorced and watched God restore his marriage while another man lost his church and God later ordained that same Pastor as a Bishop with several churches to lead.

Men who love God, follow God and serve God and are honored, not because of what they did but how they did it because they live by faith. Men do not always know what the outcome will be, but they trust God for the best outcome. Men who trust God will always experience the move of God. The way that God moves will bring liberty and satisfaction guaranteed! Men who have seen God move and accept God's will are complete and whole in him – they have nothing missing and nothing lacking!

Watch God move in the life of Richard DeShields, Jr.

My nephew Richard served as a firefighter in the Air force until May 2006. An Airman asked Richard's permission to apply for a firefighter position for him with KBR, which is a contracting company with jobs overseas. Richard was shocked when he got the job and he arrived in Afghanistan in June 2006.

Richard wanted to be his own boss. He knew that he had the Lord on his side and he was going to move in faith. He became a Real Estate Investor and purchased seven homes all together after being in Afghanistan for five years. The camp he was stationed to was getting attacked but he continued to pursue his goals. Bombs came within 10 feet in front of him and hit the living quarters next door to him killing one of his good friends. Richard said, "The Lord had his hand on me and I did not let that stop me from accomplishing my goal. It did shake me up but I stayed another year until I felt like I did enough to be my own boss."

Richard went on further to share the following: "In spite of not having a degree in real estate I was always rich in my faith and I always wanted to do what man said I couldn't. I never wanted to be a man that knew the Word but did not believe in the Word. When you believe in something you follow it and take action. Nothing in life is easy that's worth having, but you have to stand on the Word and take action and get out of your comfort zone. I like to let my actions speak louder than my words."

He furthered shared this, "When you are rich in your faith you look at everything different. I look at everything as an opportunity to relate to other people to show Jesus; I want to be an ambassador for Him. Everything that you go through in life is an opportunity to reach the nonbelievers and to inspire believers to show Jesus Christ. If you are doing everything for him then you will succeed in life because it's all about spreading the WORD. He gives us different platforms to reach everyone. The more that I do or go through, the more I can reach more people. I look at trials as opportunities. If I have to go through all this to reach one person or help someone turn there life around for Jesus Christ so they can have eternal life then it's worth it. That's what it's all about."

Richard continues to be Real Estate Investor but is enjoying helping others also as a Personal Trainer – He is a Mighty Man of Valor.

"For with God nothing shall be impossible!" (Luke 1:37)

"In the beginning God created the heaven and the earth. And the earth was without form, and void; and darkness was upon the face of the deep. And the Spirit of God moved upon the face of the waters." (Genesis 1: 1-2)

Chapter 9

Virtuous Woman

The virtuous woman is one class lady. She is clothed with so many beautiful qualities that impact her family, the community and herself. She is not perfect but every day she lived on purpose to serve God and others. She was able to both smile and laugh about her future – it looked so bright! Today we have many virtuous women on the move for God and watch God move daily in their lives. I am a virtuous woman and I love God with my whole heart and I am chasing after Him.

A virtuous woman has fortitude. She is strong in the Lord and shows courage in the midst of her pain or adversity. Many women today have experience pain that almost wiped them out, but God stepped in and gave them endurance to make it another night. Some women have experienced domestic violence, financial difficulties, problems with their children and more but they have displayed a backbone no matter what problems have come their way. Your response is a major key to overcoming any test or obstacle. Virtuous women respond with wisdom, kindness, love, and fairness and if they make a mistake – they seek God for guidance and don't look back.

A virtuous woman is a leader. She knows how to handle business and she provides good business. She gets up early but she will stay up late to get the job done. You may see her lights still on while others are still sleep. She cares about others in need and will serve them with gladness with joy and satisfaction. Every time she turns around she sees the hand of God moving in all her situations. She fears God and adores God – not for what He does but for who He is. When she feels alone and she doesn't know which way to turn, she knows how to trust God at all times and continues to be steadfast in all her responsibilities.

I get joy from serving others and God moves each time. I remember when I wrote the vision for the transitional home for abused women and their children as a special assignment in graduate school. My professor said it was very ambitious and signed it with an A. I got discouraged and doubted God, but it made me more determined to implement and plan the vision. I started with no money, no volunteers and no homes but with God ordering my steps I was able to get two homes donated. One home was licensed as a transitional home, secured and I wrote two grants without any grant writing experience, and *I'm Free Ministries* is still moving forward today. One of the grants was for a mentorship program for children who witnessed domestic violence. I dedicated this ministry to God and He continues to get the glory.

Your vision will have victory and impact other people lives for the better. If He can do it for me – He can do it for you. Write your vision and run with it. God will bring it to pass and sustain it! Watch God move!

A virtuous woman will experience God healing her body, opening doors that no man shut, keeping her mind stable and her heart whole. She definitely declares what a mighty God we serve! God has moved on her relationships, moved on her job and moved in every area of her life. A virtuous woman can be single and can abstain from sex. A virtuous woman has temperance and will exercise self-restraint and deny flesh to keep her covenant with God. I have personally seen God move in my life in this area and He has given me the courage to say no which represents my worth and the valuable gem that He has created me to be as a single woman of God.

They that wait on the Lord shall renew their strength. God has changed me – he slowed me down and I think more before I act. Every decision has a consequence and my desire is to please God first. When you make God first the right man will come into your life and the right opportunities will too. When you give God your heart, satisfaction is guaranteed and a virtuous woman you shall be. Celibacy takes discipline and the challenges will come, but you will be victorious and feel so complete in God.

I'm not sure what you are going through at this present time but I want to encourage you that God is right by your side. He knows your beginning and your end. A virtuous woman is a surrendered woman – God wants you completely – He wants your all. It's His will not our will. When you allow God to be the pilot on the plane, you will make a successful landing and nothing shall separate you from His love. You will soar into your destiny and reap a harvest for the Kingdom. There is no limit to what God can do for you, but you must always remain available to Him!

Watch God move in the life of Elder Diane Matthews

The Lord wanted Diane to start a ministry, which was birth in 2010, (Young Ladies in Transition - Women of Purpose). When she accepted the call she began to go through trials and testing. Her body was under attack during this year.

She was diagnosed with Urinary Cancer. She was fearful and in disbelief, but she sought God in prayer, and began reading healing scriptures. She went for hysterectomy surgery on May 4th (her birthday of that year) and when they went in to perform the surgery, it could not be done because a tumor was discovered on her bladder; the surgery was postponed until the end of May.

During the weeks of waiting for the surgery, she had to wear a colostomy bag to collect urine. She also experienced very heavy bleeding and was in and out of the emergency room. She had to take medication for treatment of a blood clot that developed from the earlier procedure. She was allergic to the medication which caused her to break out in hives. She continued to seek God in prayer and others were praying too.

The morning of her second surgery, the surgeon said that

there would be an Urologist to assist with the surgery to remove the tumor on the bladder. She was told there was a chance that she would have to wear colostomy bag the rest of her life.

Diane stated the following: "When I returned to my room my family was their waiting for me, with excitement. My doctor informed them that there was no tumor on the bladder - it just was not there – unexplainable, and the hysterectomy was successful!" This was a miraculous move of God for a virtuous woman!

For with God nothing shall be impossible! Luke 1:37

"In the beginning God created the heaven and the earth. And the earth was without form, and void; and darkness was upon the face of the deep. And the Spirit of God moved upon the face of the waters." (Genesis 1: 1-2)

Chapter 10

Watch God Move

God can do anything but fail. He is all knowing, all loving, all powerful and so amazing! Every time you turn around you will see God moving in some way.

Miracles happen every day – you may not know when He is going to move or how, but He will come through for you.

He delivered me from a domestic violence situation, he healed my body from a tumor, he stopped evictions, blocked shut offs, kept a roof over my head, placed money in my hands when my account was empty – I can't even explain how He did what he did, but I know God moved!

I got hit by a tractor trailer, 3 times the size of my car and walked away from the accident alive. God will protect you from dangers seen and unseen and there is nobody like Him and nobody greater! I was in the court room waiting for my eviction hearing for my apartment without any money and the judge said case dismissed; the representative from the management staff did not show. God moved! I was in a networking meeting and we were instructed to announce one of our needs and I announced the need for my rent payment, and someone got up and wrote me a check in the amount of the rent and more. God will provide all your needs according to His riches in glory! I was told by my doctor that I had a tumor and although I was nervous, I prayed and believed God for complete healing; when I returned to the doctor he reported the tumor was gone! Watch God move!

Ten means testimony and so this is another glimpse into my story. I had a fear of writing and as I share in this last chapter of this book, God has moved fear out of the way and has allowed me to do something that I once did not have the courage to do. Somewhere in my life fear creeped in and tried to cripple me, but every now and then God will send someone in your life, to help you detox all those things that is not like him. God will remove every negative experience of things that people said or done, and what was once a mess or a hindrance God will use it for His glory! As I reflect on this experience the first thing that comes to my mind is the butterfly – anything that had me crawling is over and now I have my wings to fly – my life has been transformed into this beautiful butterfly and I'm soaring high. In spite of everything that has tried to stop this book from coming forth – it is now in your hands because I placed it in God's hands. Anything you give to God – he will use it for His glory. He will take nothing and turn it into something special and beautiful, and that is my prayer for you today. Whatever your goal is – whatever your dream is – it will come to pass – there is nothing too hard for God!

As much as we want to see God move there is a process that we all must go through, even if we have to crawl like the caterpillar, you will still get to your destination with God, but you must make some moves too. Sometimes God will move when you move because faith without works is dead. (James 2:26)

The following are the 10 things that you must do: Live, Love, Fast, Pray, Have Faith, Trust God, Wait, Watch God move, Praise God and tell God Thanks!

The scripture tells us that the thief cometh not, but for to steal, and to kill and to destroy: I am come that they may have life, and that they might have it more abundantly. (John 10:10 KJV)

God wants you to be vigilant but He also wants you to live a life full in Him – nothing missing and nothing lacking. The enemy will come but He can't stop God. There is no competition with God. You win no matter what – so enjoy your life and find a way to celebrate each day and what God has blessed you with.

Be content because there is someone else in the world that maybe going through something that is worse than you. You will be tested and tried, but you will come out with a praise and another testimony of how God moved in your life.

Be wise but gentle and keep your armor on for you are not alone. And if you find yourself in a low place, allow God to lead you to still waters and comfort you for trouble don't last always!

Love will lift you daily for the love of God is like no other. And now these three remain: faith, hope and love. But the greatest of these is love. (1 Corinthians 13:13 NIV)

Oh how I love Jesus; love on Jesus daily. Love yourself. Stop beating yourself up!

Be confident of this very thing, that he which that began a great work in you will perform it until the day of Jesus Christ so love who you are and become stronger in him. Know that this may not happen overnight, but you are on your way. (Philippians 1:6 KJV)

You also must love others like God loves us. In spite of us, our hang up and mess ups – He still loves us and He wants us to operate in the same way.

Fasting and Praying is the key that will unlock breakthroughs and blessings. You have to sacrifice with a fast and give up something that you love or like and do understand it does not have to be food – it may be watching TV or being on Social Media all day and every day, but no matter what you choose to give up know that it will be worth the sacrifice.

Fasting will deliver you, it helps you to hear from God and God will honor the sacrifice and move on your behalf.

Always pray without ceasing about people and situations that concern you. God will answer. His Word tell us so in 2 Chronicles 7:14 – "If my people, which are called by my name, shall humble themselves, and pray, and seek my face, and turn from their wicked ways; then will I hear from heaven and will forgive their sin and will heal their land."

God word also states this: "Now faith is the substance of things hoped for, the evidence of things not seen." (Hebrews 11:1) You may not be able to see it or hear it, but God is going to do it! And He will be on time, and everything will be alright. It shall happen – so write that vision, make it plain, run with it and finish strong! Don't worry about the time – don't be anxious for nothing – God is going to do just what He said. He can do the impossible! Be it unto you according to God's Word!

"Trust in the Lord with all thine heart; and lean not unto thine own understanding. In all thy ways acknowledge him, and he shall direct thy paths." (Proverbs 3:5-6) Trust God even when you don't understand, trust him when it hurts or even when you are glad. Stand on His promises for they are sure and you will always remain safe and secure! Our God is faithful and He will not fail!

"Wait on the LORD: be of good courage, and he shall strengthen thine heart: wait, I say, on the LORD." (Psalm 27:14) You may not have everything you need right now – but help is on the way – resources are on the way – God is on the way to meet every need, He will dot every "I" and cross every "T." If you are single you are worth the wait – if you are married God is going to turn that marriage around – if you are sick – he will heal your body – your wait will not be in vain – you have the victory in Christ Jesus!

Watch God move! Your blessing has arrived. It is signed, sealed and delivered by God. You have done all you can do and God has now shown up for you and shown out. The best thing you can do right now is bless His name and say thank You Lord.

"Bless the Lord at all times: his praise shall continually be in your mouth." (Psalm 37:1) Be grateful for His support, thank Him for caring, thank Him for keeping you and for protecting you. Thank Him for healing you and making all your dreams a reality. Thank Him for helping you to reach that goal and thank him for being God. He is "I am that I am" so thank Him for all the things He has done both great and small.

"Lord we thank You. We give You total praise!"

Watch God Move in the life of Minister Jerri Flippen

Minister Flippen wasn't sure if she was going to make it home because she got ill. The pain in her abdomen was extremely severe as she navigated the traffic on the turnpike. She was about 90 minutes from home and was anxious to contact her doctor. When she reached for her cell phone to plug into her car's phoning device a beeping error message signified no connection.

She said, "This had never happened before!" Feeling very sick and in desperation, she picked up her phone to make the call and the next thing she recalled was flashing red and blue lights in her rear view mirror and sirens blaring. She had no doubt that she was being pulled over and prayed a prayer for mercy to the Lord.

The ticket she received demanded a court appearance. While waiting to face the judge in court that day, she called a friend for prayer; not only did her friend pray mercy for her, but mercy for everyone in court that day!

Min. Flippen shared the following: Facing the judge, I agreed to the charge of using a handheld device, but added, "…with extenuating circumstances…." The judge leaned back to listen. As I explained what happened, the judge did something remarkable! She said, "I'll talk to the prosecutor on your behalf, you may have a seat."

"What? The judge was going to speak to the prosecutor on my behalf….! I was astonished."

"Subsequently, summoned by the prosecutor into her private office, she asked me to plead guilty to a lesser charge but before I could respond she told me never mind – stating because the Judge spoke to her on my behalf, she was going to dismiss the entire matter! When I deserved judgment, I received mercy." Only God can cause your adversary to be at peace with you. **Watch God Move!**

Poem of Encouragement

Watch God Move by Arnita DeShields

I can see the breaking of day, that God is making a way!
Watch God Move!
Whatever changes must come, stand tall and hold on - life will come with many test, but with God, He will keep you at His best-never settle for less.
Watch God Move!
The money maybe at a low, but God knows and will meet every need, just watch it flow, stay strong and believe, and it will grow!
Watch God Move!
Sickness and disease will raise its ugly head, but God will deliver and heal just like He said!
Watch God Move!
People will come and people will go, but one thing will never change – His presence will always remain!
Watch God Move!
Don't worry no matter how hard it looks – your dream will come true, because God paid the price, just for you.
Watch God Move!
Nothing is impossible with God - I pray that miracles, signs and wonders will follow you, because you believe, that God will come through!
Watch God Move!

Watch God Move - 10 Day Journal

Write down daily how God has moved in your life and express your gratitude to Him!

Day 1 – The Storm Is Passing Over

There will be a shelter to give shade from the heat by day, and refuge and protection from the storm and the rain. (Isaiah 4:6)

Lord I praise You - thank you for keeping me in every storm of life, guide me and order my steps daily in your light in Jesus name I pray. Amen!

Day 2 – The Power of Prayer

And whatever you ask in prayer, you will receive, if you have faith.
Matthew 21:22

Lord I adore You – thank You for listening and for hearing my humble cry – move on every area of my life, bless my family and friends too, and meet all their needs according to your riches in glory in Jesus name I pray. Amen

Day 3 – I'm Still Standing

Put on the full armor of God, so that you will be able to stand firm against the schemes of the devil.
Ephesians 6:11

Lord I exalt You – touch every weak area in my life – give me strength to stand no matter what comes my way – cover me with your love and protect me from all harm in Jesus name I pray. Amen!

Day 4- Don't Quit

I can do all things through Christ which strengthen me. Philippians 4:13

Lord I glorify You – thank You for helping me to overcome obstacles and reach my goals – renew my mind and keep me focus in Jesus name I pray. Amen!

Day 5 - Letting Go!

Casting all your anxieties on Him, because He cares for you. 1 Peter 5:7

Lord I magnify – I turn over every concern that I have – I am letting go so that you can move by your Spirit and your will be done in my life – I surrender all in Jesus name I pray. Amen.

Day 6 – I Got Joy!

Clap your hands, all peoples! Shout to God with loud songs of joy!
Psalms 47:1

Lord I exalt You – take away any sadness & fill me with your joy – create in me a clean heart and renew a right Spirit in me in Jesus name I pray. Amen!

Day 7 – Our Children Have A Voice

Train up a child in the way he should go; even when he is old he will not depart from it.
Proverbs 22:6

Lord I praise You – bless our children – keep them on the right track – birth their dreams and help them excel always in Jesus name I pray. Amen!

Day 8 – Mighty Men of Valor

And the angel of the Lord appeared unto him, and said unto him, The Lord is with thee, thou mighty man of valor. Judges 6:12

Lord I honor you – thank you for raising up men to be conquerors – stir up their gifts and talents and use them for your glory in Jesus name I pray. Amen!

Day 9 – Virtuous Women

Who can find a virtuous woman? For her price is far above rubies.
Proverbs 31:10

Lord I adore you – thank you for developing women after your heart – crown their heads with your glory – mold them, make them and let goodness and mercy follow them in Jesus name I pray. Amen!

Day 10 – Watch God Move

For I know the plans I have for you, declares the Lord, plans to prosper you and not to harm you, plans to give you hope and a future.
Jeremiah 29:11

Lord I exalt you – thank you for the awesome plans for my life – remove all fear and doubt, and give me an opportunity to share my testimony in Jesus name I pray. Amen!

Prayer of Salvation

That if thou shalt confess with thy mouth the Lord Jesus, and shalt believe in thine heart that God hath raised him from the dead, thou shalt be saved. Romans 10:9

If you would like to get saved the following is the prayer that you can say right now:

"Lord Jesus, I believe that you died on the cross for me. Take full control of my life. Help me live each day in a way that pleases you. I love You and I thank You that I will spend all eternity with You in Jesus name I pray. Amen."

Watch God Move in the life of Arnita DeShields

On September 9th, I was in another car accident. I had just left a meeting finalizing my first book club presentation, when I was hit from the rear by someone who was high or either intoxicated. In addition to him hitting my car, he walked over and placed his hand on my waist when I got out my car. I addressed him for his behavior and got back in my car, understanding the condition that he was in. He then left his car running with cell phone in it, walked down the street, and leaped on the hood of another moving car. I prayed for him and gave God thanks for once again saving my life, and for not allowing the drivers in front of me to be harmed in any way.

My faith has been tested, my car was totaled, but God has moved each time! I can't tell it all in one book, but God continues to write my love story, and He will do the same for you! "For I know the plans I have for you," declares the LORD. "Plans to prosper you and not to harm you, plans to give you hope and a future. (Jeremiah 29:11 NIV)

Your faith will be tested, but your story will never end in defeat! Thank You for purchasing "Watch God Move". Please write me or e-mail me about how God has moved in your life. I'm praying for you and remember always, that you have the victory!

Special Thanks to everyone who shared excerpts in "Watch God Move" about how God has moved in your life – It does not yet appear what you shall be! Love and blessings always to Tina Scott, Tyre Brant and Elder Emma Brant, Dorothy

Goins, Ty Ryans-Mease, William and Tamika Haynes, Dale Croxton, Sharrod Williams, Richard DeShields, Jr., Elder Diane Matthews, and Minister Jerri Flippen.

About The Author

Arnita DeShields is currently the CEO of DeShields Counseling, Life Coaching & Consulting Services and is the Founder of Butterfly Empowerment Services Transform (B.E.S.T.) – services for abused women and their children.

Arnita is the producer and host of New Beginnings Prayer Outreach Television Ministry that will equip people with the Word of God and empower with prayer.

Embracing a passion for helping victims of domestic violence, community development, outreach and empowering individuals in all areas of their life, Arnita has been practicing social work and counseling since 1987. She serves her community as a leader and member of Camden County Commission for Women, a member of the Senior Advisory Council for the Aging, Church Health Liaison for Virtua Health System and a member of Delta Sigma Theta Sorority, Inc. Faithful in service as a volunteer, Arnita assists victims of domestic violence and is the Founder of I'm Free Ministries. Through ministry she provides housing and supportive services for victims of domestic violence and their children located in Lindenwold, New Jersey. She was awarded the Dr. Martin Luther King Freedom Medal for her dedication to community service.

Arnita has been active in a variety of Christian ministry for 24 years and is currently a member of Mount Olive Baptist Church in Philadelphia under the leadership of Pastor Harry Moore, Sr. She was licensed as a Minister on February 15,

2004 by Bishop David G. Evans of Bethany Baptist Church headquartered in Lindenwold, NJ, where she served as an Associate Minister. Arnita has preached and taught for both adults and youth at churches, conferences, retreats and seminary. She is grateful for awesome leaders that covered and mentored her in ministry.

In 2006, she started New Beginnings Radio Ministry on WTMR 800AM in Camden NJ and had re-emerged in 2009 on Radio One's Praise 103.9, Philadelphia's inspiration station. In 2007, Arnita became Co-Host of Battle for Life, a prayer outreach TV ministry that aired on the Virgin Island, New Jersey and Pennsylvania. In 2011 she became the host of New Beginnings Prayer Outreach TV Ministry presently airing on The NOW Network on Channel 16.4, every 2nd & 4th Saturday at 10pm, in Upstate South Carolina, North Carolina, Northern GA and streaming. It is a ministry designed to encourage believers and non-believers alike through exhortation and intercessory prayer "on the air" and with lessons from God's Word on how to let go of the "old" and embrace the "new", and how to avoid getting trapped in "what is", instead of positioning one's self toward "what can be" . . . Theme is "Remember Every Day Is A New Beginning" - 2nd Corinthians 5:17.

Arnita DeShields is a 1999 graduate of the University of Pennsylvania School of Social Policy and Practice, where she received a Masters of Social Work, and is also a 1990 graduate of Villanova University, where she received her Bachelor of Arts & Sciences; her major was Communications. Presently, she is attending International Miracle Institute for a

Doctorate in Christian Theology.

Arnita was born and raised in Philadelphia, PA, where she currently resides with her son, Joseph Emmanuel. She is also referred to as Lady, which is a nick name given to her from birth in honor of her late Grandmother, Lady Lee Oden. Arnita is so grateful for her loving parents, Mary Elizabeth DeShields and the late Ranzo DeShields. She is blessed to be the youngest of ten siblings, and loves both her family and friends dearly. She enjoys writing poetry, sharing her gift of spoken word, sacred dancing, reading and more.

Her life scriptures are Philippians 4:13 - "I can do all things through Christ which strengthens me," and Luke 1:37 - "For with God nothing shall be impossible!"

Connect With The Author

Arnita DeShields
P.O. Box 18531
Philadelphia, PA 19121

arnitadc@gmail.com

www.ArnitaDeShields.com

Links available on website for Facebook, Twitter, Instagram, Gracehope.com, Periscope and LinkedIN

Helpful Resources

1-800-799-SAFE(7233) National Domestic Violence Hotline
1-800-273-TALK(8255) National Suicide Prevention Lifeline
1-800-950-6264 National Alliance on Mental Illness Helpline
1-800-662-HELP(4357) Substance Abuse & Mental Health Services Administration National Helpline

You do not have to stay in any unhealthy situation. It's okay to ask for help and watch God transform your life from a caterpillar into a beautiful butterfly! **Watch God Move!**

About The Publisher

Dorothy Goins is the award winning and national best-selling author of the renowned novel, *A WOMAN SCORN'D*, a compelling story that reveals a deployable truth often subjected to secrecy throughout families; the issues of Domestic Violence. Dedicated and committed to the cause to help eradicate this plague in the community, Goins advocates diligently as a Change Partner with Women Against Abuse and as a Community Awareness Representative sharing as an educational awareness advocate for WAA. She has taught creative writing workshop to the women in the Sojourner's House Transitional Housing Program - (an emergency based transitional housing program) after receiving in 2008 a grant from The Leeway Foundation to fund her workshops.

Her workshops were designed around the method that "writing helps us to heal." After the senseless murder of her beloved sister-in-law on December 30, 2004—as a result of Domestic Violence, Dorothy Goins began her own national campaign speaking out against Domestic Violence; using her novel, *A WOMAN SCORN'D* as the driving force behind her message to the community. Her dedication and commitment has not gone unrewarded. She wrote for the widely distributed magazine, HAVING CHURCH FOR WOMEN, contributing as an editor inspiring features and motivating stories to this bi-monthly subscription. Goins has interviewed on numerous well known radio shows and stations which also includes a widely syndicated radio taping on the Michael Baisden show on 103.9 FM in 2008.

Goins most recent novel, *No Grace Without Mercy* has received numerous accolades from readers. Dorothy Goins is a Philadelphia based author whose writing style is both energetic and uplifting.

Founder of Xpressit Publications, Goins has established her work as an author and a publisher. She has three novels attributed to her devotion to writing. *Married Man,* her first novel still continues to be sought by readers.

Google or visit Dorothy Goins online or connect with her on Facebook, Twitter and check out her features on www.dorothy-goins.com. You may also contact her via email: womaniknow2@yahoo.com